A Revised Meta-analysis of the Mental Practice

Literature on Motor Skill Learning

Deborah L. Feltz

Michigan State University

Daniel M. Landers

Arizona State University

Betsy J. Becker

Michigan State University

Running head: MENTAL PRACTICE

Send correspondence to:

Deborah L. Feltz
Rm. 210, I.M. Sports Circle
School of Health Education,
Counseling Psychology and
Human Performance
Michigan State University
East Lansing, MI 48824

Abstract

The effect of mental practice on subsequent performance of a motor skill has been the subject of many reviews. The present review of mental practice effects differed from previous reviews by examining: (1) learning effects by means of effect sizes for pretest-to-posttest differences, (2) mental practice effects compared to no practice, physical practice, and mental and physical practice, and (3) effect sizes using more contemporary meta-analytic procedures recommended by Hedges and Olkin (1985). An overview of meta-analytic procedures is also presented. From the 48 studies identified as having pretest/posttest comparisons, the overall average effect size for all practice conditions was 0.43 $p<.05$). Analysis of categorical comparisons among practice conditions revealed that physical practice had the largest effect size followed by combined practice, mental practice, and no practice (control) conditions. This ordering of effect sizes was also found for moderating variables of task type (motor tasks) and dependent measures (accuracy tasks). None of the other moderating variables were statistically significant. These findings are discussed in relation to: (a) the conclusions advanced by previous reviewers of the mental practice literature, and (b) varying ratios of physical to mental practice for enhancing learning of motor skills.

A Revised Meta-analysis of the Mental Practice

Literature on Motor Skill Learning

Concomitant with the cognitive revolution in psychology has been the resurgence of research on mental practice. As a specific form of practice, mental practice has also been referred to as symbolic rehearsal (Sackett, 1935), imaginary practice (Perry, 1939), covert rehearsal (Corbin, 1967), implicit practice (Morrisett, 1956), mental rehearsal (Whiteley, 1962), conceptualizing practice (Egstrom, 1964), mental preparation (Weinberg, 1982), and visualization (Seiderman & Schneider, 1983). According to Richardson (1967, p. 95), "mental practice refers to the symbolic rehearsal of a physical activity in the absence of any gross muscular movements." Such covert activity is commonly observed among musicians and athletes prior to their performances. For example, when a gymnast imagines going through the motions of performing a still ring routine he is engaged in mental practice.

Since the 1930s there have been over 100 studies on mental practice. The specific research question addressed in these studies has been whether a given amount of mental practice prior to performing a motor skill will enhance one's subsequent motor performance. Unfortunately, definitive answers to this question have not been readily forthcoming. Although there are existing narrative (Corbin, 1972; Richardson, 1967 a, b; Weinberg, 1982) and meta-analytic (Feltz & Landers, 1983) reviews of the mental practice literature, the conclusions have been contradictory. There is a need, therefore, to conduct a comprehensive review of the mental practice literature using more sophisticated meta-analytic procedures and examining more study features than used in previous studies (e.g., Feltz & Landers, 1983).

MENTAL PRACTICE PARADIGMS

Most experiments on skill acquisition have been variants on a research design which employs four groups of subjects randomly selected from a homogeneous parent population or equated on initial levels of performance. These groups have been (a) mental practice, (b) physical practice, (c) combined physical and mental practice, and (d) no physical or mental practice (i.e., control). Most studies compared the performances (pre-post) of subjects who had previous mental practice to a control group that had not received mental instructions. In the mental practice group the time intervening between pre and posttest was usually occupied in sitting or standing and rehearsing the skill in imagination for a set amount of time. The members of the no practice group were simply instructed not to practice the skill physically or mentally during the interval. A more appropriate control has required members of the no practice group to participate in the same number of practice sessions as the mental and physical practice groups, but with activity that has been irrelevant to the task. Quite often, these groups were also contrasted to a physical practice group and a group receiving combined mental and physical practice. A practice period was then instituted which varied considerably in the number of trials in each practice session and in total number and spacing of trials. In combined mental-physical practice groups, practice periods involved either alternating mental and physical practice trials, mentally practicing a number of trials followed by physical practice, or physically practicing a number of trials followed by mental practice. Following this practice period, the subjects' skills were tested under standard conditions to determine whether their performance scores differed as a result of the practice condition administered.

The scope of the present meta-analytic review is considerably broader than in previous reviews. Whereas Feltz and Landers (1983) limited their review to only comparisons between mental practice and no practice, all four groups are compared in the present review. The previous meta-analytic study included only studies that had pretest scores or a control group with which to be compared. By contrast, the present review included only single or multiple group studies having pre and posttest scores. The use of pre-post designs permitted a determination of a change-score effect size for each group examined in this set of mental practice studies.

PREVIOUS REVIEWS

Research studies examining the effects of mental practice on motor learning and skilled performance have been reviewed on a selective basis. The reviews by Richardson (1967a) and Corbin (1972) included from 22 to 56 studies and provided contradictory conclusions. Richardson (1967a) reviewed studies of three types: (a) those that focused on how mental practice could facilitate the initial acquisition of a perceptual motor skill, (b) those that focused on aiding the continued retention of a motor skill, and (c) those that focused on improving the immediate performance of a skill. He concluded that in a majority of the studies reviewed, mental practice facilitates the acquisition of a motor skill. There were not enough studies to draw any conclusions regarding the effect of mental practice on retention or immediate performance of a task.

Five years later, Corbin (1972) who reviewed many other factors that could affect mental practice was much more cautious in his interpretation of the effects of mental practice on acquisition and retention of skilled motor behavior. In fact, he maintained that the studies were inconclusive and that a host of individual, task and methodological factors used with mental practice produced different mental practice results.

In a 1982 review of "mental preparation," Weinberg reviewed 27 studies dealing with mental practice. Although Weinberg noted the equivocal nature of this literature, he maintained that the following consistencies were apparent: (a) physical practice is better than mental practice; and (b) mental practice combined and alternated with physical practice is more effective than either physical practice or mental practice alone. The latter conclusion is similar to Richardson's (1967a) cautious inference that the combined practice group is as good as or better than physical practice trials only.

Another conclusion reached by Weinberg (1982) was that for mental practice to be effective individuals had to achieve a minimum skill proficiency. However, in their meta-analysis, Feltz and Landers (1983) found no significant differences between the effect sizes determined for novice and experienced performers.

It is not surprising that with all of the significant and nonsignificant findings in the numerous mental practice studies, it is exceedingly difficult in these narrative reviews (Corbin, 1972; Richardson, 1967; Weinberg, 1982) to obtain any clear patterns. The insights about directions for future research that were provided in previous reviews by Richardson (1967), Corbin (1972) and Weinberg (1982) were helpful. In the above reviews, however, the conclusions about mental practice effects may have been distorted for one or more of the following reasons: (a) too few studies have been included to accurately portray the overall empirical findings in the area; (b) only a subset of possible studies was included, leaving open the possibility that bias on the reviewers' part may have influenced them to include studies that supported their position, while excluding those that may have contradicted their beliefs; (c) although the reviewers speculated about a range of variables that may influence the effectiveness of mental practice, the style used in these reviews was more narrative and rhetorical than technical and statistical, thus making it difficult to systematically identify the variables; and (d) the reviews have ignored the issue of relationship strength, which may have allowed weak disconfirmation, or the equal weighting of conclusions based on few studies with conclusions based on several studies (see Cooper, 1979). In other words, they had a smaller pool of studies, and at that time, more sophisticated tools for research integration were not widely available. Thus, some of their conclusions may no longer be tenable.

Given the current confusion that may have resulted from the basic limitations of previous reviews, there is a need for a more comprehensive review of existing research, using a more powerful method of combining results than summary impression. The methodology recommended for such a purpose is meta-analysis, which examines the magnitude of differences between conditions as well as the probability of finding such differences.

AN OVERVIEW OF META-ANALYSIS TECHNIQUES

This section provides an overview of the concept and practice of meta-analysis, the quantitative synthesis of research findings. A brief introduction is followed by a discussion of Cooper's (1984) formulation of the process of integrative research reviewing. The effect size, as popularized by Glass (1976), is next introduced: this measure serves as an index of the effectiveness of mental practice training in our review. An overview of hypotheses tested by statistical method designed specifically for analyzing effect-size data (e.g., Hedges & Olkin, 1985) concludes the section.

Introduction

"Meta-analysis," (Glass, 1976) or the analysis of analyses, is an approach to research reviewing that is based upon the quantitative synthesis of results of related research studies. Although the idea of statistically combining measures of study outcomes is not new in the agricultural or physical sciences (e.g., Birge, 1932; Fisher, 1932), this approach was not often used to summarize research results in the social sciences until Glass (1976) proposed the idea of meta-analysis.

Glass described meta-analysis as "a rigorous alternative to the casual, narrative discussions of research studies which typify our attempts to make sense of the rapidly expanding research literature" (1976, p. 3). The book by Glass, McGaw, and Smith (1981) presents an overview of the process as it was first conceptualized. In Glass's view, the task of the meta-analyst is to explore the variation in the findings of studies in much the same way that one might analyze data in primary research. Questions of the effects of differences in study design or treatment implementation on study results are addressed empirically. Thus we avoid the practice of eliminating all but a few studies not believed to be deficient in design or analysis, and basing the conclusions of the review on the remaining results.

Some critics (e.g., Eysenck, 1978; Slavin, 1984) have claimed that meta-analysis (as it is generally applied) is little more than the thoughtless application of statistical summaries to the results of studies of questionable quality. In fact, as is true for some published primary research, some published meta-analyses are flawed because of problems in data collection, data analysis, or other important aspects. However, when thoughtfully conducted, a meta-analysis can provide a more rigorous and objective alternative to the traditional narrative review. Additionally, the development of statistical analyses designed especially for effect sizes makes the thoughtful meta-analysis a necessity rather than an option.

The Integrative Review

Both Jackson (1980) and Cooper (1982, 1984) have conceived of the steps involved in an integrative research review as parallel to those familiar in the conduct of primary research. Cooper (1984) outlines and details five steps in a research review and the "functions, sources of variance, and potential threats to validity associated with each stage of the review process" (1984, p. 12). These five stages are outlined below.

Problem Formulation

At this first stage of the review, the researcher must outline the research questions for the review and the kinds of evidence that should be sought in order to address those questions. Here the reviewer deals with the conceptualization and operationalization of constructs, the specificity versus generality of conclusions to be drawn, and the question of whether to conduct a review which tests hypotheses on the basis of "study-generated evidence" or a review which proposes hypotheses on the basis of "review-generated evidence." Study-generated evidence comprises information about effects examined _within_ studies, such as treatment effects or the relationships of critical subject characteristics to treatment effects. Review-generated evidence concerns effects that cannot be, or usually are not, tested within single studies. For example, evidence about the relationship to study results of features of research design or methodology would be review-generated evidence.

Data Collection

At this stage of the review, the issue is the identification and collection of studies. Cooper details many literature-search procedures, and discusses ways to evaluate their adequacy.

Data Evaluation

This stage of the research involves the accumulation of study results and the "coding" of study features which may later serve as explanations for patterns of study outcomes. During this step, the meta-analyst computes quantitative indices of study outcomes (representing treatment effects, degrees of relationships between variables, or other outcomes) which will later be analyzed. Also at this stage the issues of subject and treatment characteristics and study quality become crucial.

Features of the subjects (both experimental and control subjects), the treatments, and the context of the study may be related either purposely or accidentally to study outcomes. Some guidance about which features should be important will come from the problem formulation stage of the review. Important treatment features and subject characteristics that have theoretical importance must be noted for each study in order to examine plausible explanations for differences (or similarities) in study results.

Cooper describes two approaches for evaluating study quality, the "threats-to-validity" approach and the "methods-description" approach. The threats-to-validity approach involves determining whether each study in the review is subject to any of a number of threats to validity (such as those listed by Campbell and Stanley, 1963) and the methods-description approach involves the description of the features of study design via coding of the primary researchers' descriptions of the methodology of the studies. Clearly, either approach has the weakness that different reviewers may choose to list different threats to validity or methodological features, but the methods-description has the advantages of requiring fewer judgments and being more detailed (because finer details of study methods are noted).

Data Analysis and Interpretation

At this stage the reviewer selects and applies procedures in order to draw inferences about the questions formulated at the first stage of the review procedure. Different procedures are available for analyzing measures of effect magnitude such as correlations and standardized mean differences, and for analyzing probability values from independent studies. Different inferences can be based on these two kinds of analyses.

Public Presentation of Results

Finally, the reviewer must prepare the results of the integrative review for public consumption. Here issues of the amount of detail that should be reported about the conduct of the four previous stages are critical. Clearly the inclusion of every detail, regardless of its eventual importance in the findings of the review, is unwise. However, Cooper argues that the omission of details about the conduct of the review constitute a primary threat to the validity of the review.

Summary

The clarification alone of the process of conducting an integrative review has done much to enable researchers to take a more rigorous and systematic approach to research reviewing. Even so, in each review there will be special considerations suggested by the nature of the research topic or the data available that do not allow the conduct of such a review to be an automatic, thoughtless process.

Glass's Effect Size

For many years the quantitative summarization of measures of effect magnitude was not possible for much of the research in the social sciences. Glass's popularization of the effect size, or standardized mean difference, as a measure of treatment effect that could be compared across studies using nonidentical instruments or measures, was the breakthrough that allowed the broad application of quantitative research synthesis techniques in the social and behavior sciences.

The _effect size_ for a comparison between the experimental and control groups in a study is the standardized mean difference

$$g = \frac{\bar{Y}^E - \bar{Y}^C}{S}, \qquad (1)$$

where $\bar{Y}^E$ and $\bar{Y}^C$ are the experimental and control group means, respectively, and S is the pooled within-groups estimate of σ, the common population standard deviation of the scores. (Though Glass proposed using the control group standard deviation as S, Hedges (1981) noted that the pooled standard deviation is a more precise estimate of σ when the assumption of equal population variances is satisfied.)

The effect size represents the difference between the means of the experimental and control groups relative to the amount of random variation within those groups. Many reviewers discuss values of the effect size in terms of "standard-deviation units," in much the same way that a z score or standard score would be discussed. Thus, an effect size of 0.75 indicates that the means of the experimental and control groups differ by three fourths of one standard deviation. Another way to interpret the effect size is in terms of the performance of any average subject in the control group. An effect size of 0.75 indicates that the treatment implemented raises the score of the average subject three fourths of one standard deviation.

Statistical Analyses for Effect-size Data

Glass's Analyses

When Glass proposed using quantitative methods to summarize effect sizes, he argued that the effect sizes could be treated as "typical" data and analyzed using familiar procedures (e.g., ANOVA, regression). The rationale for using such analyses was that the reviewer wanted to examine variation in the results of studies, in much the same way that a researcher might examine differences between subjects in a primary data analysis. Thus, analysis of variance was used to compare results of classes or categorizations of studies, and regression was used to examine the relationships of continuous predictor variables to the study results.

Though many meta-analyses have been based on this approach to summarizing data from series of studies, including our original review of the mental practice literature (Feltz & Landers, 1983), the approach is problematic because the effect-size "data" (or the correlations or proportions) do not usually satisfy the homoscedasticity assumption required of standard statistical analyses. The variance of the effect-size estimate is inversely related to the size of the sample for which it is calculated (Hedges, 1981), and sample sizes of studies in research reviews often differ by several orders of magnitude. Furthermore, though the influence on decisions of violations of this sort has not been well studied, it seems likely to be associated with serious errors in the significance levels of tests (e.g., t and F tests) based on the analyses (Hedges, 1984). Thus, analyses designed specifically for the examination of effect-size data are to be preferred over the seemingly sensible ad hoc methods used initially.

Analyses for Effect Sizes

Analyses based on sample effect sizes allow inferences about corresponding population parameters. Hedges (1981) noted that g estimates a population effect size, δ, which may be written as

$$\delta = \frac{\mu^E - \mu^C}{\sigma}. \qquad (2)$$

The parameters μ^E and μ^C are the population means on Y for the experimental and control groups, respectively, and σ is the population standard deviation of the Y scores within the groups of the study. When the reviewer considers a set of k studies, the parameters $\delta_1, \ldots, \delta_k$ are the population values about which inferences are made when sample effect sizes are analyzed.

Though there are many similarities between the familiar analyses first employed in meta-analysis (like ANOVA and regression), and the analyses designed specifically for effect sizes, there are also differences. Statistical analyses designed specifically for effect sizes not only avoid the statistical problems of traditional analysis methods, but also provide tests of the adequacy of proposed models for the effect sizes which are not available from traditional methods. Rather than detail the statistical theory for the effect-size analyses, which is presented clearly by Hedges (e.g., Hedges, 1982a,b; Hedges & Olkin, 1985) we outline here the hypotheses that are addressed by the analyses.

Hypotheses for Effect-size Analysis

The hypotheses appropriate for effect-size data are discussed here for the context of studies comparing one experimental group to a control group on a simple posttest measure. The simplest null hypothesis for effect-size data is that all of the studies are of populations in which there are essentially no treatment effects. This is typically tested in two steps using statistical analyses for effect sizes. First, the hypothesis that all of the studies provide similar or consistent results is tested. This is the model that

$$\delta_1 = \delta_2 = \ldots = \delta_k = \delta, \tag{3}$$

where k is the number of studies being summarized. Hedges (1982a) and Rosenthal and Rubin (1982) showed how to test this model using a chi-square statistic with $k - 1$ degrees of freedom, which provides a test similar to the goodness-of-fit test from a log-linear model. Because this homogeneity test informs the reviewer about differences in the size of the treatment effect across studies, in a sense it provides a test for a "study by treatment" interaction.

If the results from all of the studies are consistent with the model of a single underlying population effect size (i.e., one treatment effect), the meta-analyst can test whether the value of that single effect (δ) differs from zero. The formal hypothesis to be tested is that $\delta = 0$. A z score is calculated by dividing the weighted mean effect size by its standard error. The test is done by comparing that sample z to a table of standard normal values.

Further Hypotheses

If the test of homogeneity for the effect sizes (model 3) is rejected and the reviewer concludes that the results are "not consistent," many alternative methods of analyzing the effect sizes are available as a next step. Many of these methods are covered in detail by Hedges (1982b,c; 1983) and others (Raudenbush & Bryk, 1985; Rosenthal & Rubin, 1982). The logic behind these alternatives is described briefly.

The goal of the alternative statistical analyses designed for effect sizes is to either "explain," estimate, or identify the sources of variability in study results. Tests for the significance of specific explanatory models are accompanied by tests for the adequacy of those models. Similarly, methods for identifying outliers provide ways to assess the impact of the omission of the outliers on the data analysis.

"Fixed-effects" analyses assume that all effect-size parameters are functions of known concomitant variables (study or sample characteristics), and thus can be "explained" in terms of an appropriate statistical model. The model may be a regression-like linear model relating predictors (e.g., sample or study features) to the effect-size outcomes (Hedges, 1982c) or a categorical model (conceptually similar to ANOVA) which posits different population effect sizes for qualitatively different sets of studies.

Other analyses assume that "random-effects" or mixed models are more appropriate for describing effect-size outcomes. The underlying assumption of these methods is that the effect-size <u>parameters</u> vary in much the same way as their sample realizations. The goal of random-effects analyses is to estimate the amount of random parameter variability in a set of outcomes. Mixed models do not obviate the possibility of between-study differences due to fixed factors. Such models simply do not presume that such fixed differences can explain <u>all</u> variability in outcomes. Thus, a reviewer using mixed-model methods might seek to reduce outcome variation via explanatory models but would not expect to <u>eliminate</u> that variation. In this approach tests of model 'adequacy' are often accompanied or replaced by estimates of residual variation in effects.

Another approach to the analysis of effect sizes, which is often combined with those mentioned above, involves the identification of outliers, or unusual effect-size estimates. Methods described by Hedges and Olkin (1985) allow the reviewer to locate studies that contribute heavily to the misspecification of proposed models for differences in effect sizes. The studies from which these estimates arise sometimes differ from other studies in ways that were not coded or thought important during preliminary data evaluation. Sometimes the features of such unusual studies can be included in a model which then explains adequately the pattern of results. Occasionally outliers are eliminated if they result from incommensurate outcome measures or because of problems in effect-size computation. The methods for identifying unusual studies can be used not only to identify problem studies, but also to identify exemplary studies.

THE NEED FOR THE PRESENT STUDY

This reanalysis of the mental practice literature will be valuable for several reasons. First, the analysis will improve upon the earlier review by expanding the set of studies investigated to include those examining a treatment featuring combinations of mental and physical practice. The Feltz and Landers meta-analysis (1983) examined only the comparison of mental practice to no practice at all.

Second, our present study will improve upon the earlier review by Feltz and Landers (1983) by using modern statistical analyses for effect sizes. Feltz and Landers employed the meta-analysis strategy initially proposed by Glass, which is problematic both because of the violation of the assumption of homogeneity of variances discussed previously, and because of the inability of this strategy to assess the adequacy of the models for differences in effect sizes. We will use the methods described by Hedges and Olkin to avoid these problems.

Furthermore, we will use the methods described by Hedges and Olkin for identifying outliers or unusual studies to pinpoint very large effect sizes. Thus, we will be able to select studies that show particularly strong mental-practice or combined mental and physical practice effects, which might serve to identify problem studies or exemplars for the design of mental-practice interventions.

Our reanalysis will also use a slightly modified version of Glass's effect size as a measure of the effectiveness of mental practice training. In their previous review, Feltz and Landers (1983) used the typical experimental versus control effect size, contrasting motor-skill performance between mental-practice and control groups.

In our reanalysis, we will use separate effect sizes for the mental practice and control groups (as well as for combined mental and physical practice groups) to represent <u>change</u> in motor skill performance. The use of this "difference-score effect size" (discussed in more detail below) will enable us to estimate not only the difference in performance due to the mental-practice intervention, but also the amount of change that would be expected for groups receiving no training or a combination of mental and physical practice. Thus, our overall null hypothesis will be that all studies show on average the same degree of <u>change</u> in motor skill for the mental practice, physical practice, combined, and control groups.

METHOD

In this section, we detail the methodology for our meta-analysis. The first section details the literature search procedures used to identify our collection of studies. Next, the definition and computation of effect-size measures, and the coding of study features are discussed. The remaining section deals with the analysis of our effect-size data. We discuss the comparisons of practice paradigms to be made, as well as other discrete (grouping) variables that may be related to the amount of change in motor skills. Then we present a rationale for the investigation of several continuous predictor variables for the amount of change in motor skill performance. Finally, we discuss our rationale and methodology for the examination of outliers.

The Collection of Studies

Study sources were obtained from the Feltz and Landers (1983) review and from a manual search of the literature subsequent to 1982. From this search we identified 60 unpublished sources, 48 of which were obtainable and 48 published sources, all of which were obtainable. This resulted in a total of 96 distinct sources that were retrieved and identified as having examined the effects of some form of mental practice on motor performance. Each article was then read, effect-size measures were extracted where sufficient data were provided, and relevant study features were coded. This procedure produced 55 studies from which effect sizes could be obtained. Of the 41 studies that could not be used, 37 did not report enough information on which to calculate effect sizes and four were not relevant to the purpose of this review.

Definition and Computation of Effect-Size Measures
Notation for a Series of Studies

Consider a series of k studies each examining the treatment effect in one or several samples. Let X_{ijl} and Y_{ijl} be the pretest (X) and posttest (Y), respectively, for the lth person in the jth sample of the ith study. If a study examines the pretest and posttest motor-skill performance of subjects in mental-practice and control groups, it has two independent samples. Denote the J_i as the number of independent samples in the ith study, n_{ij} as the sample size in the jth sample in study i, and assume that in sample j of study i, X_{ijl} and Y_{ijl} are independently normally distributed with means μ_{ij} and η_{ij} and with variances σ^2_{ij} (sigma) and η_{ij} (eta), respectively. Thus

$$X_{ijl} \sim N(\mu_{ij}, \sigma_{ij}), \text{ for } l = 1,\ldots,n_{ij}, \; j = 1,\ldots,J_i,$$
$$i = 1,\ldots,k,$$

and

$$Y_{ijl} \sim N(\mu_{ij}, \eta_{ij}) \text{ (etc.)}, \text{ for } l = 1,\ldots n_{ij}, \; j = 1,\ldots,J_i,$$
$$i = 1,\ldots,k.$$

The Difference Score Effect Size

We define the difference-score effect size as the standardized difference between the posttest and pretest means for a single sample, divided by the pretest standard deviation.

We write

$$g_{ij} = \frac{Y_{ij} - X_{ij}}{S_{ij}}, \qquad (4)$$

where Y_{ij} and X_{ij} are the posttest and pretest means, respectively, and S_{ij} is the pretest standard deviation in the jth sample from the ith study.

We define the difference-score effect size in the metric of the pretest scores for two reasons. The primary reason is interpretability. By dividing by a standard deviation of <u>scores</u> (rather than of change scores) we obtain an effect size in score units. Thus a difference-score effect size of 0.75 for a mental practice group indicates that the average subject in that group increased his or her performance by three-fourths of one standard deviation. If the skill in question were basketball jump shots, and the standard deviation of the number of pretreatment shots made was 10, then the average change is easily seen to be 7.5 additional shots made.

The second reason is that the pretest standard deviations would not be influenced by the treatments. They should be roughly equivalent across groups withing studies, assuming that subjects were randomly assigned to groups, thus large difference-score effects should not result from decreased variation in scores in groups where the treatment may have affected score variability (note influence of $\sigma^2 \neq \eta^2$ on variance of g).

The sample change-score effect size, g_{ij}, estimates a <u>population</u> effect size, δ_{ij}, which may be written as

$$\delta_{ij} = \frac{\mu_{ij}^X - \mu_{ij}^Y}{\sigma_{ij}}. \tag{5}$$

As above, μ_{ij}^X and μ_{ij}^Y are the population means on X and Y for the jth sample in ith study and σ_{ij} is the population standard deviation of the X scores within the jth sample of study i. Below we will see that the sampling distribution for the effect size is greatly simplified if we assume that $\sigma^2 = \eta^2$. Inferences are made about the k parameters $\delta_{11}, \ldots \delta_{kJ}$ when sample effect sizes or their significance values are analyzed.

Computation of Effect Sizes

Most studies provided the pretest and posttest means and the pretest standard deviation needed to compute the effect size directly, as shown in equation 1. Effect sizes were computed for as many distinct control, mental practice, physical practice, or combined mental/physical practice groups as were examined. Thus, a single source could provide any number of difference-score effect sizes. In the present review, the maximum number of effect sizes from any one source was 96 (Wills, 1966). The Wills (1966) study measured 8 outcomes for 12 independent samples of subjects. When several outcomes were studied, when single outcomes were scored in more than one way (e.g., in terms of both speed and accuracy), and when multiple test trials were reported, we computed several (dependent) effect sizes for each group. (No interdependent data are combined in our analyses, however).

When raw means and pretest standard deviations were not reported, effect sizes were computed in other ways. In two studies, the posttest standard deviation replaced the pretest standard deviation in the computation of g. In some cases, gain-score standard deviations (S_g) or t tests for change in performance were reported. In these cases g was computed via a simple algebraic identity.

$$g = \frac{(Y - X)\sqrt{2(1-r)}}{S_g},$$

using the gain-score standard deviation, and via

$$g = \sqrt{\frac{2(1-r)}{n}}\, t,$$

when n is the sample size of the group and t is the t test for change for only that group. (Note that the square root of the corresponding change-score F could also be used in place of t here.) The correlation r represents the correlation between X and Y, the pretest and posttest measures. Values of r were not generally reported, thus had to be obtained from a subset of studies which reported either the pre-post correlation or raw data (which allowed computation of r).

The values of r used for the four treatment groups were $r = +.69$ for control groups, $r = +.64$ for the mental practice groups, $r = +.20$ for the physical practice groups, and $r = +.16$ for the combined mental/physical groups. These values are the median correlations retrieved from the subset of studies which reported r or raw data. Each median r is based on a set of between seven and 10 correlations. The values of the median correlations suggest that the pretest-posttest correlation is quite strong for control and mental-practice groups. Where some intervening physical practice has taken place, the relationship is weaker; the correlations for physical and combined groups are less than one-third the size of the control and mental practice correlations.

We also computed some effect sizes by approximating the value of S_g with the pooled within-groups mean square from a gain-score analysis of variance. Thus, with this method, we used the same standard deviation for all groups resulting from one article or study. Our formula for g was

$$g = \frac{(Y - X)\sqrt{2(1-r)}}{\sqrt{MSW}}.$$

Preliminary analyses indicated, however, that effect sizes computed using this approach were systematically larger than effect sizes from studies similar in other aspects. This may have resulted because of between-group differences in variation or pretest versus posttest differences in variation which could not be detected (because the necessary variances were not reported). Six studies with effect sizes computed via this method were eliminated from further statistical analysis.

Variance of the Effect Size

Hedges (1981) presented asymptotic distribution theory for Glass's estimate of effect size. The gain-score effect size has a similar distribution. The gain-score effect size is biased, but an unbiased estimate of the population value is computed as

$$d = c(n-1)g,$$

where $c(m) = 1 - (3/(4m-1))$, and the variance of d is approximately

$$V = \frac{2(1-\underline{r})}{\underline{n}} + \frac{\underline{d}^2}{2(\underline{n}-1)}.$$

Again $\underline{r}$ is the estimated pre-post correlation and $\underline{n}$ is the sample size.

The estimate $\underline{d}$ is asymptotically normal with an expected value of δ (delta) the population difference-score effect size and a variance given by $\underline{V}$. Analyses of our difference-score effect sizes are based on those described in detail by Hedges (e.g., Hedges, 1982; Hedges & Olkin, 1985).

Coding of Study Features

Numerous study characteristics were coded for the 55 studies in the final collection. Table 1 presents a list of the study features used in our analyses.

These study features are the same as those used by Feltz and Landers (1983) with the exception of subject's sex and design characteristics as well as categories of open/closed skills. Subject's sex was not found to be important in moderating the effect of mental practice and was, therefore, not coded in our review. Because difference-score effect sizes were computed in our analysis, the design characteristics used by Feltz and Landers were not appropriate.

Types of Comparisons

Our primary comparison of interest was among the treatment groups or different types of practice. It has been theorized that combined mental and physical practice is better than either physical practice or mental practice alone (Corbin, 1972). However, this comparison has not yet been made within a meta-analysis. In addition, as was done in the Feltz and Landers (1983) review, comparisons were made by task type, publication status, subject experience, and time of posttest. Comparisons that had not been made previously were between studies using different types of dependent measures and between studies using subjects with different levels of imagery ability.

The continuous predictor variables that were investigated were number of practice sessions and number of practice trials per session or length of each practice session in seconds. Some researchers have suggested that the greater the number of mental rehearsals the greater the effect on performance (Sackett, 1935; Smyth, 1975), whereas others have suggested that there may be an optimal number of practice sessions and length of practice in which mental practice is most effective (Corbin, 1972; Twining, 1949). Feltz and Landers (1983) found no linear or curvilinear relationship between number of practice sessions and effect size; however, they did find curvilinear relationships between length of practice and effect size. Unfortunately, they were not able to determine, statistically, whether other variables (e.g., task type) moderated these relationships.

Rationale and Methodology for Outliers

Outliers were examined in the first step of the data analysis to identify unusual studies that could bias subsequent results. Confidence intervals were computed and plotted for each effect size. Unusual results were identified by examining the confidence interval plots for the separate treatment groups. The studies identified were then re-read to determine any unusual features.

On the basis of this preliminary analysis, six studies that had effect sizes computed by approximating the value of Sg with the pooled within-groups mean square were eliminated from further analysis. One study (Corbin, 1966) was eliminated because the pretest task was different than the posttest task. In addition, the Kelsey (1961) study was eliminated because it was the only study that measured muscular endurance. Consequently the physical practice sample in this study had extremely high effect sizes.

RESULTS

Overall Test of Homogeneity

From the 55 studies in which effect sizes were computed, 48 were used in our meta-analysis. These 48 studies had examined change in motor skills for 223 separate samples. A summary of the characteristics for these studies is presented in Table 2. Included in this table is an indication of random assignment of subjects to groups, whether pretreatment group differences existed, and how effect sizes were computed.[1]

We first tested the consistency of change in motor skill across 223 samples. The overall homogeneity test H_T value was 788.32, which as chi-square variable with $\underline{k}-1 = 221$ degrees of

---

[1] The effect sizes for these studies can be obtained by writing the first author.

freedom, is quite large ($p<.001$). All the change-score effect sizes cannot be represented with one population parameter. This does not seem surprising since the biased uncorrected effect sizes range from -0.38 to 13.91.

The weighted average effect size for all studies is estimated to be 0.43 standard deviations, which differs from zero ($p<.05$). This value represents the average change effect from pre- to posttest across all types of practice treatments. The value is just slightly lower than the unweighted average effect size (0.48) reported by Feltz and Landers (1983) which was computed using the mental practice versus control means rather than computing difference-score effect sizes.

Categorical Comparisons

We next grouped the effects according to treatment group or type of practice. Table 3 shows the homogeneity statistics obtained for this categorical analysis and the overall homogeneity test (Hedges, 1982b). An overall test of the within-groups homogeneity, H_W, is the sum of the homogeneity values for each subgroup. Its value, 668.69 is significant at the .001 level ($df=218$). Thus, there is still considerable variation in the sizes of change over practice within the treatment groups. The results within the four treatment categories are also not homogeneous.

The test for differences among mean effect sizes for the treatment groups is given by H_B, which is also a chi-square variable, with 3 degrees of freedom. We conclude that the four sets of pre-post differences have different population effect sizes, since $H_B = 119.63$ is significant.

Mean change differences for all of the treatment groups were significantly greater than zero with physical practice showing the greatest change effects (0.79) and, as we would expect, the control groups showing the smallest change effects (0.22). The average weighted change-score effect size for mental practice groups (0.47) is very close to the unweighted effect size reported by Feltz and Landers (1983). Contrary to what has been previously theorized in the literature (Corbin, 1972), combined mental and physical practice does not appear to be more effective than either mental or physical practice alone.

We next subdivided the different treatment groups according to task type since this was the categorized variable that Feltz and Landers (1983) found to be most significant in differentiating effect sizes. The task-type categories were motor tasks, cognitive tasks, and strength tasks. The homogeneity statistics for task type divided by treatment group are shown in Table 4. An inspection of Table 4 indicates that most of the variation in effect sizes occur with the motor tasks. The overall test of within-groups homogeneity is significant, $H_W(\underline{df}=155) = 547.74$ as well as the four treatment categories.

Since grouping the studies by task type for four treatment groups did not fully explain the variations in pre/post differences, we explored the use of another study feature, type of dependent measure used, as a grouping variable for motor type tasks. The dependent measure categories were accuracy, speed, form, distance, and time on target or in balance. The homogeneity statistics for measure type by treatment group are shown in Table 5. It appears that most of the variation in effect sizes for motor tasks is from studies using measures of accuracy or time on target/in balance.

Analyses Using Continuous Predictors

In order to determine the influence of number of practice sessions and length of practice per session, we conducted separate regression analyses for each predictor variable for each of the four treatment groups. In each regression analysis, we tested for (a) overall significance of the regression model using four polynomial predictors (linear, quadratic, cubic, and quartic), (b) the fit of the regression model (analogous to H_w homogeneity tests), and (c) Z tests for significance of individual predictors. Table 6 contains the summary statistics for these analyses.

For the number of practice sessions variable, the overall models were significant for mental practice, physical practice and combined practice groups, but the chi squares for model fit were also significant indicating a large amount of error in the models. For the length of practice per session variable which was measured in terms of number of practice trials, the overall models were significant for control, mental practice and physical practice groups with the control group having the only nonsignificant chi square for model fit. Although the control group regression analysis was significant and showed good fit, none of the individual polynomial predictors were significant using a Z test. This may be due to the multicolinearity among the predictors. Thus, unlike Feltz and Landers (1983) who found a curvilinear relationship between length of practice and effect size, we found no linear or curvilinear relationships between the continuous variables measured and effect size.

Discussion

Comparing across all types of tasks and practice conditions used in the 48 studies reviewed, the results of the meta-analysis showed that the average difference in effect size from pretest to posttest was 0.43 standard deviations ($p<.05$). Likewise, the average effect size for mental practice was 0.47 ($p<.05$). The overall learning, as indicated by the magnitude of the difference in pretest to posttest effect sizes, is of similar magnitude to the overall mental practice effect size (0.48) reported by Feltz and Landers (1983). Regardless of whether the effect size was computed using mental practice versus control (Feltz and Landers, 1983) or computed using change-score effect sizes, the resulting effect sizes represent approximately one-half a standard deviation. Considering the marked differences in types of tasks, ages, background of subjects, and research designs/methodologies employed in the studies subjected to meta-analysis, it is clear that: (a) mental practice does facilitate learning, (b) these results are replicable, and (c) they have surprisingly good generality.

When the overall effect sizes were broken down to examine moderating variables of task type and type of dependent measure, most of the variation was found in tasks that predominantly involved accuracy or tasks that were primarily "motor" in nature (versus cognitive and strength). The failure to find variation for strength and cognitive tasks, as well as speed, distance, time-on-target/in balance and form-dependent measures was most likely due to the insufficient number of samples in some practice conditions ($\underline{N} < 5$).

Examination of the categorical comparisons of practice conditions for the motor and accuracy tasks showed that the learning associated with mental practice was twice as great as that achieved from the minimal (but significant) learning demonstrated by the subjects in the no practice (control) condition. Compared to the physical practice, however, mental practice was 41-45% less effective than physical practice. These results support the general findings in the literature that physical practice is a more effective learning strategy than mental practice (Weinberg, 1982). Although some learning was achieved by the control subjects, it was 71-73% less than that achieved through physical practice.

Of particular interest in the present meta-analytic review was the categorical comparisons for the combined practice condition. Previous reviewers (Richardson, 1967; Weinberg, 1982) have maintained that a combination of mental and physical practice "is more effective than either physical practice or mental practice alone" (Weinberg, 1982, p. 203). Richardson (1967a) is much more cautious suggesting only a trend for the motor performance of combined practice to be "as good or better than physical practice trials only" (p. 103). These conclusions were not supported by the findings of the meta-analysis. Where the number of effect sizes were sufficient for legitimate statistical comparisons to be made,[2] the results showed that the effect sizes for combined practice was always less than those for physical practice. For the effect size summed across types of tasks as well as the effect sizes for motor and accuracy tasks, the combined practice was respectively 22%, 8% and 27% less than that achieved by the exclusive employment of physical practice.

It appears that overall there is a reduction in performance efficiency when physical practice is replaced by mental practice. However, there are times when such a loss may be acceptable or even desirable. For example, some motor or accuracy tasks for which actual physical practice may either be expensive, time-consuming, physically or mentally fatiguing or potentially dangerous, the small decrements in performance resulting from combined practice may be an effective teaching-learning strategy, since its effects are nearly as good as physical practice with only half the number of physical practice trials.

With only one exception (Oxendine, 1969), most of the combined practice consisted of a 50:50 ratio of physical practice to mental practice trials. In Oxendine's (1969) study, only one of the three tasks examined showed differences among the following ratios of physical practice to mental practice trials: 8:0, 6:2, 4:4, and 2:6. The 8:0 and 6:2 ratios had the greatest improvement in time-on-target scores with means of 4.37 and 4.43,

---

[2] For task measures of time-on-target/in balance, combined practice actually had a larger difference score effect size than either physical or mental practice. However, this finding is of questionable significance due to the relatively small number of samples and a much larger standard error of measurement.

respectively. With fewer physical practice trials, the scores were considerably less (i.e., 3.98 for the 4:4 ratio and 2.94 for the 2:6 ratio). Although much more research is needed to confirm these findings, it appears that the conclusions of Richardson (1967a) and Weinberg (1982) may be valid, but only if the ratio of the physical to mental practice trials is at least 75:25.

Table 1

Features of Studies

Study Feature	Categories
Treatment (Type of Practice)	Control Mental Practice Physical Practice Mental/Physical Practice
Task Types	Motor Cognitive Strength Endurance
Type of Dependent Measure	Accuracy Speed Strength Power Form Distance Time on Target Time in Balance Endurance
Time of Posttest	Immediately after practice Delayed
Subject Age Groups	Elementary High School College Adult
Subject Experience	Novice Experienced
Subject Imagery Ability	Low High

Table 1

Features of Studies (Continued)

Study Feature	Categories
Effect Size Computation	Pretest SD used Posttest SD used Gain Score SD used t test used $\overline{MS}$ within used
Study Date Number of Practice Sessions Length of Practice (Trials or Secs.) Number of Test Trials	

Table 2

Summary of Characteristics for Mental Practice Studies

Author	Year	Treatment	Age	Exper./ Novice	# Prac. Sessions	Length of Practice	Immediate Posttest
Arnold	1965	MP,PP,MPP	Coll	Nov	9	50 trials	n
Bagg	1966	C,MP	Coll	Exp	9	9 trials	n
Beckow	1967	C,MP	Coll	Nov	6	6 min	n
Bissonette	1965	MP	Elem	Exp	10	10 min	n
Burns	1962	C,MP,PP,MPP	HS	Nov	14	30 trials	n
Clark*	1960	MP,PP	HS	Nov	14	30 trials	n
Corbin*	1967	C,MP,PP	Coll	Nov	13	30 trials	n
Cronk	1967	C,MP,PP,MPP	Coll	Nov	24	10 trials	n
Dunbar	1970	MPP	Coll	Exp	4	16 trials	n
Egstrom*	1961	C,MP,PP	Coll	Nov	5	5 min	y
Eideness	1965	MP	Coll	Nov	16	25 trials	n
Epstein*	1980	C,MP	Coll	Nov	1	3 min	y
Gondola	1966	C,MP,PP,MPP	Coll	Nov	5	5 min	n
Hall*	1981	MP	Coll	Exp	5	20 min	n

Table 2 (Continued)

Summary of Characteristics for Mental Practice Studies

Author	Year	Treatment	Age	Exper./ Novice	# Prac. Sessions	Length of Practice	Immediate Posttest
Harby	1952	C,MP,PP,MPP	Coll	Nov	7,14,2	Not given	n
Howe	1967	MP,MPP	Coll	Nov	6	10 min	n
Johnson	1967	C,MP	Elem	Nov	5	5 min	n
Kelsey*	1961	C,MP,PP	Coll	Nov	20	5 min	n
Kovar	1969	C,MP,PP,MPP	Coll	Nov	6	5 min	n
LaLance	1974	C,MP,PP,MPP	Coll	Nov	8	Not given	n
Luebke	1967	PP,MPP	Elem	Nov	9	12 trials	n
Maxwell	1968	MP,PP,MPP	Coll	Nov	8	10 trials	n
McKeown	1967	MPP	Coll	Nov	18	10 trials	n
Mendoza & Wichman*	1978	C,MP,PP,MPP	Coll	Exp	12	15 min	n
Murphy	1977	C,MP	HS	Exp	12	Not given	n
Noel*	1980	C,MP	Coll	Both	4	30 min	n
Oxendine*	1969	PP,MPP	Elem	Nov	7	12 trials	n
						12 trials	
						20 min/8 trials	

Table 2 (Continued)

Summary of Characteristics for Mental Practice Studies

Author	Year	Treatment	Age	Exper./ Novice	# Prac. Sessions	Length of Practice	Immediate Posttest
Perry*	1939	C,MP,PP	Elem	Nov	5	1 min	n
						1 min	
						1 min	
						1 min	
						30 sec	
Powell*	1973	MPP	Coll	Nov	1	72 trials	y
Pruner	1971	PP,MPP	Elem	Nov	20	25 trials	n
Rawlings & Rawlings*	1974	C,MP	Coll	Nov	1	3 min	y
Rawlings et al.*	1972	C,MP,PP	Coll	Nov	8	25 trials	n
Rodriguez	1967	C,MP,PP,MPP	Coll	Nov	17	5 min	n
Ryan & Simons*	1982	C,MP,PP	Coll	Nov	1	30 sec/10 trials	y
Ryan & Simons*	1983	C,MP,PP	Coll	Nov	1	9 trials	y
Ryan & Simons*	1981	C,MP,PP	Coll	Nov	1	30 sec/9 trials	y
Sheldon	1963	MP,PP	Coll	Exp	9	5 trials	n

Table 2 (Continued)

Summary of Characteristics for Mental Practice Studies

Author	Year	Treatment	Age	Exper./Novice	# Prac. Sessions	Length of Practice	Immediate Posttest
Smith & Harrison*	1962	C,MP,PP	Coll	Nov	6	10 sec	y
Standridge	1971	MP,PP,MPP	Coll	Nov	8	30 min	y
Start*	1962	C,MP	HS	Nov	9	5 min	n
Stebbins*	1968	C,MP,PP,MPP	Coll	Exp	18	25 trials	n
Stephens	1966	C,MP,PP	Coll	Nov	6	9 trials	y
Surburg*	1968	C,MP	Coll	Nov	24	Not given	n
Surburg*	1976	C,PP,MPP	Senior Citizen	Nov	7 & 14	4 & 8 trials	n
Trussell	1952	C,MP,PP,MPP	Coll	Nov	15	5 min & 20 trials	n
Tufts	1963	MP,PP	Coll	Exp	9	15 min	n
Twining	1949	C,MP,PP	Coll	Nov	20	15 min	n
White et al.*	1978	C,MP,PP,MPP	HS	Nov	4	15 min	n
Whitehill	1965	C,MP,PP	Elem	Nov	5	5 min	n

Table 2 (Continued)

Summary of Characteristics for Mental Practice Studies

Author	Year	Treatment	Age	Exper./Novice	# Prac. Sessions	Length of Practice	Immediate Posttest
Whitehill	1964	C,MP	Elem	Nov	8	7 min	n
Whitworth	1986	C,MP	Coll	Exp	2	3 min	n
Wills, B.J.	1966	C,MP,PP,MPP	Coll,HS,Elem	Nov	6 & 8	Not given	y
Wills, K.C.	1965	C,MP,PP	Elem	Nov	15	30 trials	n
Wilson	1960	C,MP,PP	Coll	Exp	6	28 trials	n
Woolfolk et al.*	1985	C,MP	Coll	Nov	4	15 min	n

43

Table 2 (Continued)

Summary of Characteristics for Mental Practice Studies

Author	Randomized Assignment	Pre-Treat. Group Dif.	Task	Calculat. of Effect Size*	Dependent Measure
Arnold	Y	NS	Dart throw (motor)	pretest; SD	accuracy
Bagg	Y	NS	Baseball batting (motor)	pre	accuracy
Beckow	Not given	Not given	Badminton serve (motor)	pre	accuracy
Bissonette	Not approp.	Not approp.	Speed skating (speed)	pre	speed
Burns	Not given	Not given	Dart throw (motor)	pre	accuracy
Clark*	Y	Not given	One-hand free throw - BB (motor)	S gain	accuracy
Corbin*	Y	Not given	Wand juggling (motor)	t-test	number correct
Cronk	Not given	NS	Grip strength (strength)	pre	strength
Dunbar	Y	Not given	Front crawl (speed, power, form)	pre	power, speed, form
Egstrom*	Y	NS	Ball-striking (motor)	pre	accuracy
Eideness	Not given	Not approp.	One-hand free throw - BB (motor)	t-test	accuracy
Epstein*	Y	Not given	Dart throw (motor)	pre	accuracy
Gondola	Not given	NS	Base test of dynamic balance (motor)	pre	time in balance
Hall*	Not given	Not approp.	Free throw - BB (motor)	pre	accuracy

Table 2 (Continued)

Summary of Characteristics for Mental Practice Studies

Author	Randomized Assignment	Pre-Treat. Group Dif.	Task	Calculat. of Effect Size*	Dependent Measure
Harby	N	NS	Underhand free throw - BB (motor)	pre	accuracy
Howe	Not given	NS	Ball juggling (motor)	t-test	accuracy
Johnson	N	NS	Handball serve (motor)	pre	accuracy
Kelsey*	Y	NS	Sit-ups (strength)	pre	endurance
Kovar	N	NS	Underhand free throw - BB (motor)	pre	accuracy
LaLance	N	NS	Handball serve (motor)	pre	accuracy
Luebke	N	NS	Overarm SB throw (motor)	pre	velocity
Maxwell	N	NS	VB serve (motor)	---	accuracy
McKeown	Not given	Not approp.	Triple jump (motor)	t-test	distance
Mendoza & Wichman*	Y	Not given	Dart throw (motor)	S gain	accuracy
Murphy	Y	NS	Jump-shot BB (motor)	pre	accuracy
Noel*	Y	Not given	Tennis serve (motor)	MSe	% good 1st & 2nd serve
Oxendine*	N	NS	Soccer kick (motor)	pre	accuracy
	N	NS	Jump shot - BB (motor)	pre	accuracy
	N	NS	Pursuit rotor (motor)	posttest	time on target

Table 2 (Continued)

Summary of Characteristics for Mental Practice Studies

Author	Randomized Assignment	Pre-Treat. Group Dif.	Task	Calculat. of Effect Size*	Dependent Measure
Perry*	Y	NS	Card sorting (cognitive)	pre	speed & accur.
	Y	NS	Pegboard (cognitive)	pre	speed & accur.
	Y	NS	Symbol digit (cognitive)	pre	speed & accur.
	Y	NS	Mirror tracing (motor)	pre	speed & accur.
	Y	NS	Three-hole tapping (motor)	pre	speed & accur.
Powell*	Matched	Not given	Dart throw (motor)	S gain	accuracy
Pruner	N	Not given	Free throw - BB (motor)	pre	accuracy
Rawlings & Rawlings*	N	Not given	Pursuit rotor (motor)	pre	time on target
Rawlings et al.*	Y	NS	Pursuit rotor (motor)	MS between	time on target
Rodriguez	Not given	NS	Abdominal strength (strength)	S gain	strength-tension
Ryan & Simons*	Y	NS	Stabilometer (motor)	pre	time in balance
Ryan & Simons*	Y	NS	Motor maze (cognitive)	S gain	speed/accuracy
Ryan & Simons*	Y	Not given	Stabilometer (motor)	pre	time in balance
	Y	Not given	Dial-a-maze (cognitive)	pre	speed/accuracy
Sheldon	Not given	NS	Breaststroke (motor)	pre	speed

Table 2 (Continued)

Summary of Characteristics for Mental Practice Studies

Author	Randomized Assignment	Pre-Treat. Group Dif.	Task	Calculat. of Effect Size*	Dependent Measure
Smith & Harrison*	Y	Not given	3-hole stylus punchboard (motor)	S gain	speed/accuracy
Standridge	Not given	NS	Swimming whipkick (motor)	t-test	form
Start*	Not approp.	Not approp.	Underhand free throw - BB (motor)	pre	accuracy
Stebbins*	N	Not given	Target throw-ball (motor)	S gain	accuracy
Stephens	Not given	NS	Ball throw (motor)	pre	accuracy
Surburg*	Y	Not given	Forehand tennis drive (motor)	pooled posttest SD	Broer-Miller
Surburg*	Y	Not given	Pursuit rotor (motor)	pre	time on target
Trussell	Y	NS	Ball juggling (motor)	pre	number of catches
Tufts	Not given	Not given	Bowling (motor)	pre	accuracy
Twining	Y	Not given	Ring toss (motor)	t-test	number correct
White et al.*	Y	NS	Action-reaction swim start (motor)	MSe	judges' rating
Whitehill	N	NS	Ball throw (motor)	pre	accuracy
	N	NS	Paddleboard (motor)	pre	accuracy
	N	NS	Handball toss (motor)	pre	accuracy

Table 2 (Continued)

Summary of Characteristics for Mental Practice Studies

Author	Randomized Assignment	Pre-Treat. Group Dif.	Task	Calculat. of Effect Size*	Dependent Measure
Whitehill	N	Not given	Handball serve (motor)	pre	accuracy
Whitworth	N	NS	Rifle shooting (motor)	pre	accuracy
Wills, B.J.	N	NS	Standing long jump (strength)	pre	strength - distance
Wills, K.C.	N	NS	Hand grip (strength)	pre	strength
Wilson	N	NS	Football pass (motor)	pre	accuracy
Woolfolk et al.*	Not given	NS	Tennis forehand/backhand (motor)	pre	Broer-Miller
	Y	NS	Putting - golf (motor)	pre	number correct

Table 3

Treatment Group Differences Among Effect Sizes

Source	df	Test of Homogeneity	p	Mean effect-size estimate (s.e.)
Total	221	788.32	.001	0.43 (0.02)*
Between groups	3	119.63	.001	
Within groups	218	668.69	.001	
Control	47	116.71	.001	0.22 (0.03)*
Mental practice	68	236.54	.001	0.47 (0.03)*
Physical practice	53	148.28	.001	0.79 (0.05)*
Combined practice	50	167.17	.001	0.62 (0.05)*

Table 4

Analysis of Change in Type of Task by Treatment Group

Source	df	Test of Homogeneity	p	Mean effect-size estimate (s.e.)
MOTOR	158	681.69	.001	0.47 (0.02)*
Between groups	3	133.96	.001	
Within groups	155	547.74	.001	
Control	32	96.57	.001	0.24 (0.03)*
Mental practice	53	208.93	.001	0.49 (0.03)*
Physical practice	38	112.13	.001	0.88 (0.06)*
Combined practice	32	130.10	.001	0.81 (0.07)*
COGNITIVE	2	13.72	.01	0.95 (0.20)*
Between groups	2	13.72	.01	
Within groups	0	0.00		
Control	0	0.00		0.47 (0.24)
Mental practice	0	0.00		2.09 (0.49)
Physical practice	0	0.00		2.08 (0.49)
Combined practice	–	–		–
STRENGTH	59	54.47	ns	0.21 (0.04)
Between groups	3	5.33	ns	
Within groups	56	49.15	ns	
Control	13	16.26	ns	0.11 (0.07)
Mental practice	13	9.31	ns	0.27 (0.08)
Physical practice	13	14.36	ns	0.38 (0.11)
Combined practice	17	9.22	ns	0.18 (0.10)

Table 5

Analysis of Change in Type of Measure by Treatment Group for Motor Type Tasks

Source	df	Test of Homogeneity	p	Mean effect-size estimate (s.e.)
ACCURACY MEASURE	112	438.55	.001	0.43 (0.02)*
Between groups	3	74.94	.001	
Within groups	109	363.61	.001	
Control	26	76.57	.001	0.24 (0.03)*
Mental practice	43	154.08	.001	0.46 (0.03)*
Physical practice	22	74.68	.001	0.84 (0.07)*
Combined practice	18	58.27	.001	0.61 (0.08)*
SPEED MEASURE	8	27.48	.001	0.62 (0.11)*
Between groups	2	14.72	.001	
Within groups	6	12.76	.05	
Control	–	–		
Mental practice	2	1.67	ns	0.31 (0.14)
Physical practice	2	10.67	.01	0.70 (0.22)
Combined practice	2	0.42	ns	1.40 (0.23)
FORM MEASURE	2	1.55	ns	0.41 (0.21)
Between groups	2	1.55	ns	
Within groups	0	0.00	ns	
Control	–	–	–	
Mental practice	0	0.00		0.25 (0.27)
Physical practice	0	0.00		0.94 (0.48)
Combined practice	0	0.00		0.40 (0.42)

Table 5

Analsis of Change in Type of Measure by Treatment Group for Motor Type Tasks (Continued)

Source	df	Test of Homogeneity	p	Mean effect-size estimate (s.e.)
DISTANCE MEASURE	3	11.25	.02	0.56 (0.13)
Between groups	3	11.25	.02	
Within groups	0	0.00	ns	
Control	0	0.00		0.17 (0.18)
Mental practice	0	0.00		1.06 (0.26)
Physical practice	0	0.00		0.68 (0.30)
Combined practice	0	0.00		1.32 (0.47)
TIME ON TARGET/ IN BALANCE	29	163.91	.001	0.89 (0.07)
Between groups	3	67.77	.001	
Within groups	26	96.14	.001	
Control	4	19.44	.001	0.16 (0.11)
Mental practice	4	19.69	.001	1.34 (0.17)
Physical practice	10	20.21	.05	1.21 (0.14)
Combined practice	8	36.81	.001	1.57 (0.17)

Table 6

Summary of Regression Analyses for Continuous Predictors

Predictor Variable	df	Chi Square Model	df	Chi Square Error
No. of Practice Sessions				
Control	4	2.13	23	47.79*
Mental Practice	4	20.59*	36	84.72*
Physical Practice	4	18.74*	36	98.32*
Mental/Physical	4	15.12*	39	146.39*
No. of Practice Trials				
Control	4	17.75*	23	32.17
Mental Practice	4	37.86*	36	67.45*
Physical Practice	4	29.82*	36	87.23*
Mental/Physical	4	3.62	39	157.89*

* $p < .05$

References

Arnold, E.L.
 1965 *The relationship between physical and mental practice and initial ability in learning a simple motor skill.* Unpublished doctoral dissertation, Indiana University.

Bagg, E.J.K.
 1966 *Effect of mental and physical practice on baseball batting.* Unpublished master's thesis, University of California at Los Angeles.

Beckow, P.A.
 1967 *A comparison of the effectiveness of mental practice upon the learning of two gross motor skills.* Unpublished master's thesis, University of Oregon.

Birge, R.T.
 1932 The calculation of errors by the method of least squares. *Physical Review,* 40, 207-227.

Bissonette, R.
 1965 *The relative effects of mental practice upon the learning of two gross motor skills.* Unpublished master's thesis, Springfield College.

Burns, P.L.
 1962 *The effect of physical practice, mental practice, and mental-physical practice on the development of a motor skill.* Unpublished master's thesis, The Pennsylvania State University.

Campbell, D.T. and Stanley, J.C.
 1963 *Experimental and Quasi-experimental Designs for Research.* Chicago: Rand-McNally.

Clark, L.V.
- 1960 Effect of mental practice on the development of a certain motor skill. Research Quarterly, 31, 560-569.

Cooper, H.M.
- 1979 Statistically combining independent studies: A meta-analysis of sex differences in conformity research. Journal of Personality and Social Psychology, 37, 131-146.
- 1982 Scientific guidelines for conducting integrative research reviews. Review of Educational Research, 52, 291-302.
- 1984 The Intergrative Review, Beverly Hills: Sage.

Corbin, C.B.
- 1967 The effect of covert rehearsal on development of a complex motor skill. Journal of General Psychology, 76, 143-150.
- 1972 Mental practice. In W.P. Morgan (Ed.), Ergogenic Aids and Muscular Performance. New York: Academic Press.

Cronk, J.M.
- 1967 The effect of physical practice, mental practice, and physical-mental practice on the development of arm strength. Unpublished doctoral dissertation, Florida State University.

Dunbar, D.W.
- 1970 The effect of four designs of physical-mental practice upon the learning of the front crawl. Unpublished master's thesis, University of Maryland.

Egstrom, G.H.

1964   Effect of an emphasis on conceptualizing techniques during early learning of a gross motor skill. *Research Quarterly*, *35*, 472-481.

Eideness, C.L.

1965   *The effect of physical, mental-physical, and mental practice on the learning of a motor skill*. Unpublished master's thesis, South Dakota State University.

Epstein, M.L.

1980   The relationship of mental imagery and mental rehearsal to performance of a motor task. *Journal of Sport Psychology*, *2*, 211-220.

Eysenck, H.

1978   An exercise in mega-silliness. *American Psychologist*, *33*, 517.

Feltz, D.L. and Landers, D.M.

1983   The effects of mental practice on motor skill learning and performance: A meta-analysis. *Journal of Sport Psychology*, *5*, 25-57.

Fisher, R.A.

1932   *Statistical Methods for Research Workers* (4th ed.). London: Oliver & Boyd.

Glass, G.V.

1976   Primary, secondary, and meta-analysis of research. *Educational Researcher*, *5*, 3-8.

Glass, G.V., McGaw, B., and Smith, M.L.

1981   *Meta-analysis in Social Research*. Beverly Hills, CA: Sage.

Gondola, J.C.

1966   A comparison of the effectiveness of programs of physical practice, mental practice, and a combined physical and mental practice on the performance of a selected test of balance. Unpublished master's thesis, Purdue University.

Hall, E.G.

1981   The effect of positive visual imagery on free throw accuracy of intercollegiate women basketball players. Unpublished manuscript. (Available from E.G. Hall, School of Health, Physical Education and Recreation, Louisiana State University, Baton Rouge, LA 70803).

Harby, S.F.

1952   Comparisons of mental and physical practice in the learning of a physical skill. U.S.N. Spec. Dev. Cen. Tech. Rep. S.D.C., 269, 7-25.

Hedges, L.V.

1981   Distribution theory for Glass's estimator of effect size and related estimators. Journal of Educational Statistics, 6, 107-128.

1982a   Estimation of effect size from a series of independent experiments. Psychological Bulletin, 92, 490-499.

1982b   Fitting categorical models to effect sizes from a series of experiments. Journal of Educational Statistics, 7, 119-137.

1982c   Fitting continuous models to effect size data. Journal of Educational Statistics, 7, 245-270.

1983   A random effects model for effect sizes. *Psychological Bulletin*, 93, 388-395.

1984   Advances in statistical methods for meta-analysis. In W.H. Yeaton and P.M. Wortman (Eds.). *Issues in Data Synthesis*. New Directions for Program Evaluation, no. 24. San Francisco: Jossey-Bass.

Hedges, L.V. and Olkin, I.

1985   *Statistical Methods for Meta-analysis*. New York: Academic Press.

Howe, D.P.

1967   *The influence of five schedules of mental practice upon the physical performance of a novel gross motor skill after a criterion measure of skill has been attained*. Unpublished doctoral dissertation, Texas Woman's University.

Jackson, G.B.

1980   Methods for integrative reviews. *Review of Educational Research*, 50, 438-460.

Johnson, B.L.

1967   *An examination of some factors which might be related to effective utilization of mental practice in learning a gross motor skill*. Unpublished master's thesis, University of Oregon.

Kelsey, I.B.

1961   Effects of mental practice and physical practice upon muscular endurance. *Research Quarterly*, 32, 47-54.

Kovar, S.V.

1969   *The relative effects of physical, mental, and combined* mental-physical practice in the acquisition of a motor skill. Unpublished master's thesis, University of Illinois.

LaLance, R.C., Jr.

1974 A comparison of traditional instruction, mental practice, and combined physical-mental practice upon the learning of selected selected motor skills. Unpublished doctoral dissertation, Middle Tennessee State University.

Luebke, L.L.

1967 A comparison of the effects of varying schedules of mental and physical practice trials on the performance of the overarm softball throw. Unpublished master's thesis. University of Wisconsin-Madison.

Maxwell, J.M.

1968 The effect of mental practice on the learning of the overhand volleyball serve. Unpublished master's thesis, Central Missouri State College.

McKeown, B.C.

1967 The effect of physical, mental-physical, and mental practice on the learning of the modified triple jump. Unpublished master's thesis, South Dakota State University. (Unobtainable)

Mendoza, D., & Wickman, H.

1978 "Inner" darts: Effects of mental practice on performance of dart throwing. Perceptual and Motor Skills, 47, 1195-1199.

Murphy, T.J.

1977 *The effects of mental warm-up on jump shooting accuracy among selected boys' high school basketball players.* Unpublished master's thesis, South Dakota State University.

Noel, R.C.

1980 The effect of visuo-motor behavior rehearsal on tennis performance. *Journal of Sport Psychology, 2*, 221-226.

Oxendine, B.

1969 Effect of mental and physical practice on the learning of three motor skills. *Research Quarterly, 40*, 755-763.

Perry, H.M.

1939 The relative efficiency of actual and imaginary practice in five selected tasks. *Archives of Psychology, 34*, 5-75.

Powell, G.E.

1973 Negative and positive mental practice in motor skill acquisition. *Perceptual and Motor Skills, 37*, 312.

Pruner, S.W.

1971 *The effects of three methods of practice on improving the performance of a modified free-throw by sixth grade girls.* Unpublished master's thesis. North Texas State University.

Raudenbush, S.W. and Bryk, A.S.

1985 Empirical Bayes meta-analysis. *Journal of Educational Statistics, 10*, 75-98.

Rawlings, E.I., & Rawlings, I.L.

    1974   Rotary pursuit tracking following mental rehearsal as a function of voluntary control of visual imagery. Perceptual and Motor Skills, 38, 302.

Rawlings, E.I., Rawlings, I.L., Chen, S.S., and Donis Yilk, M.

    1972   The facilitating effects of mental rehearsal in the acquisition of rotary pursuit tracking. Psychonomic Science, 26, 71-73.

Richardson, A.

    1967a   Mental practice: A review and discussion. Part I. Research Quarterly, 38, 95-107.

    1967b   Mental practice: A review and discussion. Part II. Research Quartlery, 38, 264-273.

Rodriguez, G.J.

    1967   A comparison of the effects of mental and physical practice upon abdominal strength in high school girls. Unpublished master's thesis, University of North Carolina at Greensboro.

Rosenthal, R. and Rubin D.B.

    1982   Comparing effect sizes of independent studies. Psychological Bulletin, 92, 500-504.

Ryan, D.E., and Simons, J.

    1981   Cognitive demand, imagery, and frequency of mental rehearsal as factors influencing acquisition of motor skills. Journal of Sport Psychology, 3, 35-45.

    1982   Efficacy of mental imagery in enhancing mental rehearsal of motor skills. Journal of Sport Psychology, 4, 41-51.

1983   What is learned in mental practice of motor skills: A test of the cognitive-motor hypothesis. <u>Journal of Sport Psychology</u>, <u>51</u>, 419-426.

Sackett, R.S.

1935   The relationship between amount of symbolic rehearsal and retention of a maze habit. <u>Journal of General Psychology</u>, <u>13</u>, 113-128.

Seiderman, A. and Schneider, S.

1983   <u>The Athletic Eye</u>. New York: Hearst Books.

Sheldon, M.F.

1963   <u>An investigation of the relative effects of mental practice and physical practice in improving the efficiency of the breast stroke</u>. Unpublished master's thesis, University of Oregon.

Slavin, R.E.

1984   Meta-analysis in education: How has it been used? <u>Educational Researcher</u>, <u>13</u>, 6-15.

Smith, L.E., & Harrison, J.S.

1962   Comparison of the effects of visual, motor, mental and guided practice upon speed and accuracy of performance of a simple eye-hand coordination task. <u>Research Quarterly</u>, <u>33</u>, 299-307.

Smyth, M.M.

1975   The role of mental practice in skill acquisition. <u>Journal of Motor Behavior</u>, <u>7</u>, 199-206.

Spears (Alexander), C.L.

1966   <u>The effect of mental practice and physical practice in</u>

learning the running high jump for college women. Unpublished master's thesis, Arkansas State College.

Standridge, J.O.

1971   The effect of mental, physical, and mental-physical practice in learning the whip kick. Unpublished master's thesis, University of Tennessee.

Start, K.B.

1962   The influence of subjectively assessed games ability on gain in motor performance after mental practice. Journal of General Psychology, 67, 169-172.

Stebbins, J.

1968   A comparison of the effects of physical and mental practice in learning a motor skill. Research Quarterly, 39, 714-720.

Stephens, M.L.

1966   The relative effectiveness of combinations of mental and physical practice on performance scores and level of aspiration scores for an accuracy task. Unpublished master's thesis, University of North Carolina at Greensboro.

Surburg, P.R.

1968   Audio, visual, and audio-visual instruction with mental practice in developing the forehand tennis drive. Research Quarterly, 39, 728-734.

1976   Aging and effect of physical-mental practice upon acquisition and retention of a motor skill. Journal of Gerontology, 31, 64-67.

Trussell, E.M.

    1952   Mental practice as a factor in the learning of a complex motor skill. Unpublished master's thesis. University of California at Berkeley.

Tufts, S.A.

    1963   The effects of mental practice and physical practice on the scores of intermediate bowlers. Unpublished master's thesis, University of North Carolina at Greensboro.

Twining, W.E.

    1949   Mental practice and physical practice in learning a motor skill. Research Quarterly, 20, 432-435.

Weinberg, R.S.

    1982   The relationship between mental preparation strategies and motor performance: A review and critique. Quest, 33, 195-213.

White, K.D., Ashton, R., and Lewis, S.

    1978   Learning a complex skill: Effects of mental practice, physical practice, and imagery ability. International Journal of Sport Psychology, 10, 71-78.

Whitehill, M.P.

    1964   The effects of variations of mental practice on learning a motor skill. Unpublished master's thesis, University of Oregon.

    1965   The effects of mental practice on children's learning and retention of gross-motor skills. Unpublished doctoral dissertation. University of Oregon.

Whiteley, G.

    1962   *The effect of mental rehearsal on the acquisition of motor skill.* Unpublished diploma in education dissertation, University of Manchester, 1962.

Whitworth, P.

    1986   *Effects of internal imagery and experiental state on the performance of intercollegiate smallbore rifle shooters.* Unpublished Master's thesis. Department of Physical Education, Western Kentucky University.

Wills, B.J.

    1966   *Mental practice as a factor in the performance of two motor tasks.* Unpublished doctoral dissertation, University of Wisconsin, Madison.

Wills, K.C.

    1965   *The effect of mental practice and physical practice on learning a motor skill.* Unpublished master's thesis, Arkansas State College.

Wilson, M.

    1960   *The relative effect of mental practice and physical practice in learning the tennis forehand and backhand drives.* Unpublished doctoral dissertation, State University of Iowa.

Woolfolk, R.L., Murphy, S.M., Gottesfeld, D., and Aitken, D.

    1985   Effects of mental rehearsal of task motor activity and mental depiction of task outcome on motor skill performance. *Journal of Sport Psychology, 7*, 191-197.